'*Passerine* takes us through a liminal year of grief, rage and wonder, asking what do we hold onto when there is no-one there? Writing repeatedly to 'Dear Sophie' is a way of keeping the memory of a much-loved friend alive, helping the writer herself stay on the side of life, while also willing the planet, against the odds, to survive. In Sophie's absence, it is the world that speaks—through its Ten Thousand Things, notably birds, flowers, found text, interiors and the many marvellous incarnations of clouds. The language of these compelling poems is fresh and fierce, fuelled by intense looking and questioning. Every element of the book expresses passion and vivacity, endurance in the face of the unendurable: a strong dose of medicine for our troubled times.'

Linda France

'Luckins takes us on a mesmerising journey through loss, grief and healing, through landscapes where time and perspective are in turns darkened and illuminated by the natural world, its wildness and unpredictability. The language is startling, cinematic; everyday detail is revealed in a new and brilliant light. Every poem will touch a nerve. This is a remarkable collection that establishes Luckins as a poet that can speak to your soul.'

Jane Lovell

'Like all great experimenters, Kirsten Luckins is freed rather than bound by self-imposed restrictions, and this remains true in her third collection *Passerine*. This collection captures the stages of grief over a year through letters filled with nature, studding her reflections with tactile and fiercely witty imagery. *Passerine*'s an elegy not just to a lost friend but to a world that is rapidly disappearing around us—one of the most dazzling collections I've read in a long time.'

Claire Trévien

PASSERINE

Kirsten Luckins is a poet, performer, and creative producer who lives on the North East coast, as close to the sea as possible. Her practice is centred on poetry but driven by playfulness, collaboration and experimentation, so encompasses film, collage and text art, performance and theatre-making. She has toured two award-nominated spoken word shows, and worked as dramaturg to many poets and projects, including the award-winning *The Empathy Experiment*. She is artistic director of the Tees Women Poets collective, and co-founder of the Celebrating Change digital storytelling project where she teaches creative memoir writing. *Passerine* is her third collection.

Passerine

Published by Bad Betty Press in 2021
www.badbettypress.com

Cover design by Amy Acre

Printed and bound in the United Kingdom

A CIP record of this book is available from the British Library.

ISBN: 978-1-913268-13-8

LOTTERY FUNDED | Supported using public funding by
ARTS COUNCIL ENGLAND

Passerine

Kirsten
Luckins

PRESS

For Sophie Cannet
1975 – 2016

Passerine

Contents

POLLEN

Dear Sophie,	17
Dear Sophie,	18
Dear Sophie,	19
Dear Sophie,	20
Dear Sophie,	21
Dear Sophie,	22
Dear Sophie,	23
Dear Sophie,	24
Dear Sophie,	25
Dear Sophie,	26

PYRE

Dear Sophie,	29
Dear Sophie,	30
Dear Sophie,	31
Dear Sophie,	32
Dear Sophie,	33
Dear Sophie,	34
Dear Sophie,	35
Dear Sophie,	36
Dear Sophie,	37
Dear Sophie,	38
Dear Sophie,	39

GREEN GHOSTS

Dear Sophie,   43
Dear Sophie,   44
Dear Sophie,   45
Dear Sophie,   46
Dear Sophie,   47
Dear Sophie,   49
Dear Sophie,   51
Dear Sophie,   52

THE NIGHT INSIDE OUR CHESTS

Dear Sophie,   55
Dear Sophie,   56
Dear Sophie,   57
Dear Sophie,   60
Dear Sophie,   61
Dear Sophie,   62
Dear Sophie,   64
Dear Sophie,   65

COMETLIGHT

Dear Sophie,   69
Dear Sophie,   70
Dear Sophie,   71
Dear Sophie,   72
Dear Sophie,   74
Dear Sophie,   75

THE CLIFFS AT THE EDGE OF THE WORLD

Dear Sophie,	79
Dear Sophie,	80
Dear Sophie,	82
Dear Sophie,	83
Dear Sophie,	84
Dear Sophie,	85
Dear Sophie,	86
Dear Sophie,	88
Acknowledgements	89

Pollen

Dear Sophie,

30th May

The clouds today are high and scant, a promise
of heat haze and pollen count.

My mother has a cold, and is afraid of dying.

Below her thinning skin, capillaries burst
at the slightest provocation.
Her arms blotch with brown-maroon bruise,
damson rotten under the foxing.

All our mothers are afraid of dying.

Veins rope over the backs of their hands
like aerial roots. All our mothers
become jungle temples.

In Europe, my mother walked every day
in the heat, through thundery air
and the scent of mock oranges.
Genus philadelphus, a friendly plant. Once,
they were the favourite flowers for bridal coronets. Once,
all our mothers had first to be brides. Imagine!

Sweet, white stars fastening
those gauzy veils like scanty clouds
that must be lifted for life to begin.

Dear Sophie,

4th June

The clouds today are storm-leavings, rapid indigo-ash, bruised from unspent rain. I know the sparrows wake at 4am because here I am, watching them furtle through the branches of their tree. In the dawn I am *voyeuse, voyageuse, voleuse, volante, vol.* Today I leave this sky for another. The clouds stomp along with their heads down, commuters to another town's forecast.

Dear Sophie,

7th June

The clouds today are the trailing fronds of the whole white sky as it rolls up the glen.

Here sits silence,
         come for me, but my body is louder.

Open the bones, what is inside?
         More sleep.

Birdsong taps my shoulder when I stray as I often do into a past slipping past like trainseen fieldswet with buttercupsblunted by black cows and the bluewhitegrey factories against the bluewhitegrey raining I thought yes it's all very well the powerof yes the flyingof yes the running up the coaxingchiding of the hidden yes the shaking of shiny things in the eyeline of no the plumping of life's cushions yes it'sallverywell but

Sophie?
         I don't feel very well.

Dear Sophie,

8th June

The clouds today are precarious heaps, broken by sun into flocks of witless cumuli. I walk to the lake; slow as a banyan grove; every step careful of terrain; of bog; of the firm black and sloppy khaki of old and new sheep shit.

Since the Buddha-tree blew down in January, someone has built a labyrinth of river-rocks.

All is poetry, without me, or with. It's only the stepping-towards that makes it so. Only the standing-with. Only the listening-for.

Once we lay together on our backs, on the summer grass in Heaton Park, and the watching-together of the overhead clouds was a being-with. Each other. Pain. Guilt. Your womb a nest made of bird-bones, hollow and feather-light as a brown passerine.

It was always yours to fill; always yours to empty.

Dear Sophie,

9th June

If I ever use the word   *petrichor*

just shoot me.

Dear Sophie,

10th June

The clouds today were peach blossoms massed behind the forest ridge, but that was dawn, like a fall of rhododendrons, and once the fever left me I went back to bed.

I've not seen the sky since, but the darkling light and the fitful slamming of my window tells me the heavy great stratus are back, ready to rain on lawn and loch and courting wagtails.

The Dharma says that an apple tree will never become an oak, but may in time become a better apple tree.

I have lived in hatefulness and rage for more than a year now, and no sign of acorns, I can assure you.

Dear Sophie,

11th June

Peaceful as
panes pressed
by flowers

in the common
room, the
knitters name
their stitches

it's all Greek to
me

iris pseudacorus

A pale yellow
flag opens like
three sisters
spun from the
same

A *rosa gallica*,
'Sophie's
Perpetual'
grows to 5ft,

myth of fates

ideal for all soils

Dear Sophie,

12th June

Between the courtyard and the community house, a desire line runs up the grass, a silvering. Buttercups spring at its margins where the grass is still low. Then they are lost in the clouds of wilder sedge, where the grass-heads swap their empurpled braids of seeds, shake their tassels and candelabra. The meadow is the skyline of a fantastical theopolis, an abundance of spire and stupa. Fat black slugs coil through the stems as gravely as Doges. Damselflies hover above, slivers of turquoise both steady and swift. As I write this, black flies the size of rice grains land on the pages, tuck back their wings—transparent, triangular, banded with thin black bars like leaded windows. Stretching my legs to go look into the mouths of the golden lilies, I see they are also visited by flies. A rush hour of tiny bodies taking the escalators down into the depths of the flowers, they swarm and clog the beautiful with their hungers and their needs.

Dear Sophie,

13th June

I'm just looking. Everything looks like something else. Am I always hoping for a sign? Rap on the table. Blow the candle out.

What images in your notes may in fact be symbols that are speaking to you?

Flies; paths; horses. The direction 'up'. The word 'Sophie'.

How might this inform questions you have about your life today?

Dear Sophie,

29th June

I don't know how to bear it
other than by turning away.
I didn't really want it,
I never loved you anyway.

The clouds today are absent,
the sky brutally dry.
Only the 6am windows are misted
with the breath
of the sleeping rosemary outside.

Nightmares about poems
have brought me to this, sitting in the dawn
longing for dusk,
when the garden will be filled with a fury
of dust-brown moths,

whirring minims of night air
that pirouette on flower-heads.
Like me they will itch
for the coming dark.

Pyre

Dear Sophie,

2nd July

The clouds today roll smartly right to left, a hoop bowled by a high-up breeze. It occasionally drops into the garden, quick as a goldfinch. Then, the vine shakes its clamour of elastic arms. Then, the cherry tests one heavy leaf at a time. Along the back fence, the roses turn as brown as washing-up foam slurried with grease. But the gothic oxalis has decided to thrive, and the fuschia is churning out ballerinas. I read a poem where a man leaves his job to stand in a cathedral of trees, which is nice, but who will pay the electric?

Dear Sophie,

10th July

The clouds today are the last few sweepings
from an old ladies' hair salon.
The sea breeze lifts curtain into flag.
Odd modernist chorus of gull and Hilux ignition.

North of me, tall ships are moored in the mouth of the Wear,
their complicated sails all rolled up like a coalman's ciggy.

I greatly desire to tramp again around the curved hip of the coast,
watching those ships unfasten themselves into the wind.

Did you ever see your mother's hair turn white?
I think she always dyed.
The fits had streaked you grey too early,
but you never cared.

Your hair would have been a pennant today,
as usual signalling
        I want to communicate with you.
Never   *I am leaking dangerous cargo.*
Never   *I am dragging my anchor; I require*

medical assistance.

Dear Sophie,

27th July

The clouds today are the colour of dust. I look at them with the sun
already burning, and I can smell the old Misermatic firing up its
three electric bars. Its metal boxing was a pitted brown, flecked with
paint-spittle from all the times the mantel was tarted up or toned
down again. Like us, this house survived the seventies. Looks like it
may see the end of days. I am bitter as a crunched lemon pip stuck
in a molar, a curse on the world and all who drown in her. I'm eating
bread and jam again, forbidden fruit; I love it like a blues song.
Reaching for poems, I'll end up capsizing the dresser. We'll be left
with a square tureen and one oval serving platter. You'll say to me *at
least these are the most generous members of the service*, and then you'll
show me how to make a mosaic of the rest. *Une muraille de coraille.*
Smashing.

Dear Sophie,

5th August

At 2am my skin was a tarmac road wobbling the air with heat. Fifty fires were burning above the Arctic Circle, they were a tyre necklace flaming, and all the birds dropped from the skies like Vietnamese monks. The sun tightened its cincture and the equator ignited. The cradle of life reinvented itself as pyre, and out of immolation came the future, demanding an explanation.

Dear Sophie,

6th August

The clouds today are a collage of leftover ticking. We must make our goals smaller, but incessant. This is part 5,672 in the quest to learn perseverance. My mind flurries about within the walls of my skull, harassing me like a toddler. I will lie upside down on the sofa and decant my thoughts. Through the open door the garden glows darkly in the thunderlight. I will wait for the change in air to touch my hair with forgiveness. I swear to you now as I did then, it is not God who ratifies the intercessor, the channel opens wherever you place your trust. Priestless, we forgive each other. Your wrists pulse in my thumbs. The walls yellow as lilies. Years ago in our futures, only a bus ride away, the clouds are waving and rolling, rolling and waving, like babies too young to sit up.

Dear Sophie,

11th August

When he is wounded
and close to death,
Tolstoy's hero lies
collapsed on his back,
staring up at the sky.
The clouds roll over him,
and the battleground
strewn with corpses.
They roll over the
death-cries of the
defeated, and the
celebrations of the
victorious. On and on
they roll. *The world only
asks us to love it*, he
realises. *The world is
easy to love.*

For love of birds, I chase
cats from the garden.
Still no wren this year.
Severed head, cloud-
burst of feathers, claw
lacuna on a back
doorstep. The storm
winds have punched
holes through migrations.
Thousands of passerines
have fallen short,
arrowheads slackening,
dropping through clouds
into the charnel house of
the Mediterranean. Tiny
birds flocking to the
drowned hands.

Dear Sophie,

12th August

Night after night your son wailed,
      and your aunt took him from you.

She bottle-fed him so that you could
      poison your breast milk with meds.

Don't fuck it up, Soph, don't fuck it up now, with your
      treacherous neurons and your poor grasp of

How Things Are Done.

      You *jongleuse*,
      You clown,
      You sprite on a unicycle,
      You ramshackle Pan,
      You piper of slum-kids,
      You scrumper of over-hanging mangoes.

No mangoes here, only the green match-heads
      of grapes on our indefatigable vine.

I hope they ripen. Not for my sake, but for the blackbirds', who
      puffle with pleasure when they eat.

I hope there are still pleasures where you are, or else
      that you are blown out completely.

He is growing up so blond without you.

Dear Sophie,

20th August

here is a drowned spider
in the bottom of the mop-bucket and now
I've seen it
I can't unsee
its sodden legs
limply spiralled
around its body like
a whorl of black hair a kiss-curl
escaped
from a little girl's braids

there is a difference
between *raising a family* and *breeding*
as our newspapers well know

across Europe the heatwave presses
down on our cold-adapted hearts
simmers our blood
reduces it as thick as thermal muds

our spirits are sent wandering into nightmare

Dear Sophie,

25th August

above the courtyard at dawn golden clouds race
fine as neural lace nebulous they change rapidly and
continuously as a thought-stream it is too early for sounds
to have woken we walk out in single file
obedient
snow clings between the sandstone blocks of the dockside
traces of it lie cupped in the worn hollows where the black
iron mooring rings are hammered in
a chill breeze touches our cropped hair grown back a little
to a brown-gold fur it pulls gently on the blue cotton hems
of our shifts you are ahead of me as they walk us to the
sheds the rickety wooden floor slopes towards the
greenish-black canal stained hanks of straw scattered
everywhere kicked outwards from the wads that mulch up
against
the feet of the stakes a pile of children
are already sliding slowly into the water under
their own dead weight holes between their glass eyes
there is no time to hold your hand
we are cattle we are not considered sentient enough for
friendship though they perceive our fear
and enjoy it
now it is time now
I hear the shot

Dear Sophie,

26th August

Rains have mangled the sky, and someone has hung it out to dry. My heart staggers out through my eyes. Simple kindnesses fill me with the precarious peace of an unbroken swimming pool, which is one vision of heaven. I leave a coffee in the till for the homeless man. When I pass him again, he is helping a foreigner find their way, his finger tracing lightly over the surface of a tourist map. The city is spread over his knees like a fresh, colourful blanket.

Dear Sophie,

21st September

The sky today has behaved so rightly,
so blue-and-whitely, so deftly Delftware,
so pompadour and pom-pom,
so gambol and shearling since the storm.

I was walking in the sky
where it lay on its side
in the leftover waves,
when five oystercatchers passed by me low,
in formation tight as a tortoiseshell.

A boy-band pivot,
a flash of natty chevrons,
and just like that
it was autumn.

Green Ghosts

Dear Sophie,

3rd October

The skies are the grey of a sparrow's breast. Our sparrows roost, then suddenly sling themselves off the tree like leaves in a gale. From clinging, to flying. Here on the side of the quick, I prune the rose and it sticks bright green middle fingers up at me. What flowers could you push up, now your hands are finally still as tubers? How in earth will you talk? I open my window the better to hear the irregular drip of old rain from the gutter-jungle, hanging around, accumulating its diamond self like a glass gourd, distending until it must break the tension and fall.

Plink.

Extended silence while it learns to bulge again.

Perhaps flying rises in sparrows like this?

Perhaps leaving was your raindrop?

Dear Sophie,

9th October

The clouds today are the blue-black of eye bags. The trees blaze against them, rebels to a sapling. Pointillist berries transport the green shadows with scarlet. The haws are set, thumb-prick carmine, and the sloes are blue as ravens.

Along the old embankment, crowds of rosebay have withered to a froth of seed-split pods swaying on rattles of madder leaves.

The grey wind.

Long-vacated, you melt into the arms of the earth, sockets deep as inkwells.

In twelve years, the scientists say, the damage will be irreversible. Your son's lifespan, again.

A break in the clouds reveals the trees are full of shadow-puppets. They tell folktales about the beginnings and ends of worlds.

In the 3 years since this was written, that estimate has fallen to 6–18 months.

Dear Sophie,

All over Europe, the men who know the old ways are boiling holly bark for half a day. They are stashing the mash in the dark for a fortnight. It is traditional.

They are pounding the paste and washing off the spelks. They are fermenting for days before they heat it with nut oil. It is traditional.

They are painting the wires and the perching boughs. They are waiting for the wintering flocks to arrive, bodies exhausted but somehow still edible. Twenty-five million silenced songbirds, brittle feet cemented in birdlime. It is traditional.

The men sing to their children *je te plumerai les pieds*. This is how their children learn about body parts.

Dear Sophie,

12th October

They say the human soul weighs twenty-one grams, though the experiment was flawed. We accept

it not as fact, but as poem. A tidal breath from the crackling black depths of the lungs

might tip the scales as much. Equivalent to coughing up the head of a blown rose

or four wooden clothes pegs, or twenty-seven buttons in shades of mauve, or a flight-stripped

ortolan bunting. Once recovered, the bird weighs a soul plus a teaspoon of sugar.

Force-fed in darkness, it doubles and bloats, until the gentlest touch snaps its throat. Roasted,

it is eaten whole. When I think of you, I always end up thinking about the birds.

Dear Sophie,

16th October

Passerines are perching birds,
Recognisable from their feet.
Their grip is automatic,
Unaffected by their sleep.
The oldest global group of them
Are called the *Corvides*,
And sat upon their special branch
Of the taxonomic tree   are:

Whistlers & bellbirds
Whipbirds & butcherbirds
Boatbills & wedgebills
Painted berrypickers

Tillers & currawongs
Figbirds & ploughbirds
Vangas & ifrits
Tiny jewel babblers

Shriketits & drongos
Fantails & apostlebirds
Ioras & boubous
Birds-of-paradise

Woodswallows, flycatchers
Ravens, crows & blue jays
And here the Bornean bristlehead
Is tentatively placed

(P.S. This is a bit of fun for your boy)

Dear Sophie,

20th October

If only I could fly, I could grab a handful of those clouds
to knit a baby's blanket. If only I could knit.
You could make a set of juggling balls out of six balloons and a kilo
of rice. You could make a boy
out of prayer, and a home out of necessity.
Still, your body evicted you nightly
at the end of a cattle prod. You were your own hostile environment.
If charity begins at home, I say
home must be made bigger. Now we are cloddishly falling from the
continent, perhaps it's for the best you are in safer ground. If you are.
I don't know.

If buried, you have un-   become;

if burned,

you

clouded.

c   l   o   u   d   e   d

    c   l   o   u   d   e

d   c   l   o   u   d   e

    d   c   l   o   u

d   e   d   c   l   o

u   d   e   d   c   l

o   u   d   e   d   c   l

    o   u   d   e   d   c

    l   o   u   d   e   d

    c   l   o   u   d   e

d   c   l   o   u

d   e   d   c   l   o

u   d   e   d   c   l

o   u   d   e   d   c   l

    o   u   d   e   d   c

    l   o   u   d   e   d

    c   l   o   u   d   e   d

        c   l   o   u   d

        d   e   d

Dear Sophie,

Sky as poison jar. Sky as linen. Sky as nothing at all.

My shoulder blades sink like pyramids holed under the waterline. *May I be happy*, I mantra, meaning, may I desire nothing at all. On the vine the green grapes stare their shade at me, hard little eyestones. They know I desire everything, though you can't take it with you. I dreamt I was a human-shaped thing, but judged faulty, my speech-chip corrupted, my feet unable to grip. Three tonnes of feathers won't budge my heart.

In Pharaoh's tombs they found unguent jars
still fragrant with cinnamon and mastic.
Burroughs was buried with a joint, and a swordstick.
Oh, and a fedora!
Warhol with a bottle of Estée Lauder.
Leonard Bernstein took a lump of amber.
Some horse tribes left bird-grain in their burial chambers.

Dear Sophie,

1st November

The clouds today are a palomino's flank. He has one mystical blue
eye. *Allons-y!*

Horses often mean poems, when they appear in poems about horses.
When they appear in fields, they mean nothing at all.

As the shutter of the month falls, I roll under and reach back
through the narrowing gap for my hat. I am a goddamn hero. I am
as good as bareback. *Allons-y!*

Another month opens, for me.
Poems gallop in the distance.

The Night Inside Our Chests

Dear Sophie,

9th November

A whiteout of rain.
The fairground packs in silence, drives away

as if to a funeral.
They leave behind green ghosts

the shape of floor-plans.
I dream of an avenue of prayer-wheels.

They scream because they want to go faster.
We have grown up

to be ruinations to our children.
I dream of revolutions.

Are dreams the wind
flapping in the prayer flags?

I dream that my comforts
will continue without end.

My heart says
I should have dreamed better dreams.

Dear Sophie,

14th November

A sunspot
        sharpens a shadow on the gate
making me see
            both shadow
                    and gate.

You sit on the old sofa.
The leather arms cool under your skin.

A sunspot
        through the yellow curtains
making me see
            you
                are
                    made of gold.

The weather changes.
Clouds
take away the gold
and the gate.

Can we talk about the dark that's coming?

Dear Sophie,

10th December

Sometimes I am a dead seed
rattled by griefs. Then
I am a bridge in high winds,
hawsers plucked. Tremors
thread my innards.

Did I seem braided steel to you?
Be honest, did I ever strike you as load-bearing? These and other
high-sided questions
slew across both lanes.
Will we ever have a leader who loves us?
Are they really eating rats in Caracas?

M&S are trying to sell me stew as a superfood.
Lloyds will give me what my GP won't, but
fees apply.
Should I tell the pharmacy guy?
About the thing that lurches
through the back of my head?
I wave lists, I dangle podcasts.

Insufficient.
The Eater of Hope on its hundred ickle feet
is making slurry of my chocolate-coated me-time.
It wants it wants it wants to know

answers to questions more shameful than these.

Dear Sophie,

20th December

Like the year, I've reached a black spot around which to pivot. Advent melts on my tongue, overly-sweet.

Giving is one pleasure of this season; but another is retreat.

The cherry tree wrings its naked hands. Tannin-brown leaves steep its feet.

I prefer to give to those who never ask; a species of retreat.

What would we talk about now, if midwinter closed the gap and let us meet?

A chisel-strike of bird alarm. I rattle the door, the black cat beats a specious retreat.

Both of us always acted about as fatherless as aphids.

How I feel is, I feel, quite resistant to speech.

Dear Sophie,

We bring a little piece of forest into our home, dress it in lights so it won't release the wolves. It dreams of the dark heart of fairy tales. When we come downstairs to wake it, it stains the grey light green. This morning I had to push the living room door back against a stiff weight of snow. Hieroglyphs of birds tracked all the way to the washing machine. Snowflakes drifted down from the ceiling rose, and the sofabed was hoary with frost. I thought I saw a distant campfire in the thicket by the bookshelves, but it was only the TV's standby light. If I can make my creaking way, I'll open the back door and all the cats will be unable to resist. They will place their little hunting paws onto the snowdrifts and follow the stuttering promise of birds into the resinous dark. And I will let the little forest deal with them.

Dear Sophie,

15th January

In the night inside our chests, our lungs ignite sparklers
and draw thin petals on to the dark.
This is how we are chrysanthemums.

Sometimes the petals we draw are feathers.
Our diaphragm plucks them from the wings of the air, so
we house a humming firebird
while we shop, and fight, and worry.

Last night I held my feather-petals
tight, driving home between blacked-out fields.
I had been to a theatre made of soft earth.

The players leapt, and looped their breath,
until the roof burst open,
confessing all the stars of the Serengeti.

Caught between three languages, you
would have been fluent in their vocabulary
of tussle, spin, and bodyjoy.
You would have known
the crawlspace under the tongue,
the signal box of the shoulders,
the flag-code in the arms.

Europe gave us a gift of you,
precious other,
building lean-tos against us
on this speckish island.

I drove watching the moon slip
down the sky like a drunken grin.

I hardly knew myself
by the time I got home to the mirror
where I keep my eyes.

Dear Sophie,

18th January

I have you in front of me now, in your hospital bed, one white cotton strap pushed down from your brown shoulder where you've just been trying to nurse him. His face is an imperious pucker in his grandmother's arms. You are looking at him as if he can't possibly be true.

Dear Sophie,

Down from the blueblack sky
come small variations to roost,

little folds of darkness dropping
to join the night caged in the tree.

Now is the time a lamp might illuminate
a mother giving a 3am feed.

I sit until the houses lumber in
to comfort me, like heifers

placing their bouquet of faces over the fence.
I once knew a man who imagined God

as a kindly cow, as milk;
but he broke my heart.

From the fissure I grew a new woman,
and she is the child I feed.

Cometlight

Dear Sophie,

19th February

There is nothing outside myself but darkness,

      in which one lit room floats. A shift-worker,

ironing a shirt in her aquarium.

      A little light makes us all feel less alone.

Be a light, I tell myself.

I saw a famous comet hang in the icy air

      above a mountain village. The night

was blacker than a lost memory. Doused houses,

      small against the starfire, and the tang

of cometlight high as a fingerbell.

      It will not come again in anyone's lifetime.

Be a light.

Dear Sophie,

4th March

There's a leaf-dank ginnel of clart from Ebor Lane to Oakworth. Cobbles slick and treacherous under the mud. All between the alder, beech and oak, drystone walls are made wetstone. Sopping tippets of lime-green moss. Catkins a carillion of tassels. The white sky dropping snow parachutes between the trees, swansdown kiss-hush in the clearing, *isles flottantes*. There's no use pretending you were anything more than human.

Heaven is a hearth fire at the other end of sleet, strong tea in pint-pot mugs. A discreet scallop to the tablecloth. To get in you must open the thickly-brown-glossed door, pressing down the spatulate thumb-plate of the old, old latch. More of us could name the stages of grief than could anatomise this lock.

Is it pointless to name the parts of an ordinary life? There was a day. There was another. We were alive, and didn't dwell on it. Time flowed quietly when our backs were turned. We moved from hour to hour like a checklist.

Dear Sophie,

15th March

Drat this poetic hush! Hey Soph, what's with all the deathiness? A starling is picking over last summer's lobelia for nesting. He looks like a sealion with his mouth full of whiskers. Hold on, I must milk my tea.

Back! And so are the tulips, joybombs detonated in underground bunkers. Asparagus season, so I think constantly of your masterly vinaigrette. Who knew salad could have a recipe? ☺

Last night I made a soup so thick it gobbed at me, like that bald gammon at the bus stop the day we were meant to Brexit. While I stirred (the soup, I mean) I heard the blackbird singing, like a muezzin calling me to evening.

Hope to hear from you soon. The sky and I continue vaguely blue.

Dear Sophie,

17th March

This cloud! explosion! silk in the sky! then

in the forest of my carpet a thread of legs, orange-gold,

whippy millipede?   turning on dust-

motes zippily, nokia snake!

I centre me crown to ground, sceptre, column, but, what is

the centre of the centipede?

when all segments of self are belly to down-drag? when

spineless?   what core?

A confusion, breach for me, no clear, nor into anything

quite.

In comes a catch to harbour, so fully the silk sky becomes

gulls, circling? not circling,   but

drawing a stacked incline of triangles, lifting one corner

each go-around fly-by, slowly riffling pages, in collective

upflight this new, tight,   one entity?

Seen close, god-eyed, every solid thing is   this,

solid is molecules square-dancing in void, edge of space

defined by invisible   motions,

even you. You! Carbon!   with grace

you too are a mile-high monopod

gliding   in the wake of fishing boats

Dear Sophie,

20th March

early – gulls freefly in skeltermobs through so little light –

glitches – white forms forming from black, and I think –

kissed awake by the chemical bath – a mind a darkroom –

archaic – in the future all metaphor will be digital

but we will persist in the lust to shoot the moment to

mount and gloat – we will have our life and see it –

instantly – nothing need wait for darkness in order to

arrive – manifesting slowly as a dream recalled – there was

a party – you were there – we sat around a fire-pit of

broken pavements – you were looking for *marrons glacés*

– I can't remember – what happened next – images of

images – in this gull-light I can't make – out the shapes –

I thought – I saw –

Dear Sophie,

31st March

May the mothers be happy.
May the pregnant be happy.
May the broody be pregnant.
May the barren re-route.
May the unhappily pregnant have their choices
                                    respected.
May the children be wanted.
May the children be not poor.
May the mothers be seen, kindly.
May they be forgiven.
May the mothers of the heart be all of the genders.
May the mothers be excused from motherhood.
May the mothers love their dead.
May the dead mothers be kissed upon their
                                    gravestones.
May the mothers be many other things.
May the children be released.

The Cliffs at the Edge of the World

Dear Sophie,

2nd April

Dot dash dot dash

... ---. --. ....

The clouds telegraph TATTY SPRING IS HERE STOP
ALL HELLEBORES & ACCELERATED WEEDS STOP
BLACKBIRDS BRAWL LIKE FLUNG CUTLERY
DRAWERS & EVERYTHING WANTS TO LAY EGGS
BUT ME   STOP being dead and come back like -.. .-.. .- -.-.
-.- -.... --- .-. -. come back like -- --- -. .-... .- -.-- if you must just
STOP

Dear Sophie,

23rd April

The weather has been pure joy for so many days it's beginning to look like mania, or an **Eco-plot To Ruin Easter Sunday, Blasts Kill 150,** billionaire's agony at 25 degree ROAST leg of lamb is a classic! In other news, Benin's agriculture has had a good season, but it wasn't easy.

What are the major threats? I buy a cut-price Easter egg, a tray of mixed lobelia, and some Factor 50. (Preparation's half the battle.) Climbers are brought in to protect Notre Dame from the elements, a lost Bob Marley is rescued from hotel basement, and **Charles begs for an end to this pervasive horror.**

Meanwhile, all the local pigeons fuck on my bathroom windowsill. **Saudi Arabia executes 37,** Trump accuses Twitter, and the **Shadow Of Death Is Cast Over Easter.** Weeding in the shade, the cherry reaches out a petalled hand so soft and clammy-cool I mistake it for a revenant. Oil prices surge.

What are the major threats? In tinderbox conditions, the army drop slings of water onto wildfire. The government advises Yorkshire to club together for their own helicopter. (Preparation's half the battle.) My sister-in-law sits in the gloaming, watching the mountains around her burn like a **Knife Crime Blitz.**

With Farage On Course, I remember that Hitler was once a laughing stock. In Whitby, the animatronic Dracula fleeces tourists with the promise of fictional horror. (I haven't seen that in a while.) Smashing an avo for brunch, if I look weepy, it's **The Greta Thunberg Effect.**

Dear Sophie,

What with the unseasonable highs and the constant demands to sort beans from gravel, these days my mood ring is permanently the colour of summer piss. If I were Snow White the bluebirds would have done this shit for me.

Mum's gone private to buy a bit more eyesight, says she's spending my inheritance. *You have to see!* I say, glad she probably won't be around to see me evacuate her herbaceous borders for survival tatties and the kale of the coming apocalypse.

O! Convenience! What a brutal god you turned out to be. Kali only wanted the blood of black goats, but it looks like you won't be happy until we've slaughtered every last creature on the planet.

Dear Sophie,

27th April

I want to tell you about an installation by Andy
Goldsworthy called 'Outclosure'...

We enter a large, circular pen, built of drystone &
twice cut
at top & tail, for walkers like us – a lure and
        a let.
Inside the pen's parentheses grows an ugly copse,
bound close
(a tangle of birdsong, rout of roots & rot)
& inside that (the target's gold) another wall, a keep,
        a core.
No part loose, no slot for eyes, too high, no holds for
toes.
What's inside? The stone heart closes us out,
        a ruse
to make us nose the tearspot blooms of lichens for
clues,
& speculate that god, or truth, is present there – but
we're not sure.
Despite the subtle compass of its weathering, we
are lost.

Dear Sophie,

30th April

The clouds tonight are savage mixtapes,
suffering vibrations.
They are bittersweet narratives,
wandering plights.

The garden blooms saintly confessions,
a bleached archipelago of tulips.
White-headed foetus gospels,
I'll have to lift them,
every year they dwindle,
such bored reissues.

The sky bundles the moon
into its priestly flour sack.
I go back to my dreams,
those blurred pastiches,
those powerless attempts.

Dear Sophie,

2nd May

If there were only a way to hold it all;
the lit and unlit windows of the night,
the desks and checkouts of the day.

Across the lap of the Alps, a cyclist
grips the wound cloth of her handlebars.
A fan of tendons articulates the effort
of the climb, her sweat a holy oil.

In a red house in a hollow of snow
the height of a child, ten years old,
a father puts a milk pan on the stove.
The world smells of smoke and wet wool.

On the shining autobahn, a man opens
his engine to dangerous limits, feeling how
his wings spread wide as a condor, the song
on the radio close to ripping him apart.

In the TV, a woman cries over spilt power,
and cathedrals, her martyr's train lifted
by three thousand unaccompanied minors
in pageboy outfits of rubble-grey.

On a bare bones beach, a smart woman
collects shells with her grandson, until
it's time to go. I've seen them, and so
now I must remember to love them too.

Dear Sophie,

5th May

I stepped ashore one May night, the waters warm around my ankles, the shingle crunching underneath my keel. *In the cool moonlight* the low, bulbous cliffs were illuminated, their folds and fossa thrown into black relief. I looked for the slim crevice *where grass and flowers were grey* camouflage for the near-invisible entrance that would lead me deep inside the rock. *But the scent was green* of the sea all upon me, confusing me, sealing my breath, and the sounds, the inky sloshings, were turning me from my bearings. Had I gone too far? *I glided up the slope* of the beach, clambered over boulders and slipped clay patchy with salt turf *in the colourblind night,* calling a soft hoo-hoo into every dark nook, listening for the deeper echo calling back, *while white stones signalled to the moon* from among the cobbles, treacherous as search beams. *A period of time a few minutes long, fifty-eight years wide had kept us apart.*

Had the land fallen over our meeting place, this cleft I couldn't find no matter how I scrambled? *And behind me, beyond the lead-shimmering waters,* sailed, dark and silent, the armada of those who would separate us still, bearing down on my wake. *Was the other shore and those who ruled* there destined to imprison me forever? Would I fail to find this final key to my escape? This was my last hope to elude those jailers, those *people with a future instead of a face,* all looking to their fame and the next rung on their ladders, forcing my chin up likewise. All mocking my desire for this one true meeting, in the caves under the cliffs at the edge of the world.

Italicised lines by Tomas Tranströmer

Dear Sophie,

30th May

What more can I possibly tell you?

Here are the white stars of iris-lilies. Here are the
tumbled pots.

I follow the clouds down the coast. They are so
charismatic, both dark and radiant at once.

At North Gare, something rises in me as elementary and
banal as a skylark over a golf course.

A sudden wind silvers the marram pelt. The scrub ponies
come galloping to forage my pockets.

They carry white stars on their brows.

Acknowledgements

Thanks are due to the editors of *Butcher's Dog, Capsule Stories, Fly on the Wall, Ink, Sweat & Tears, Pure Slush* and Black Light Engine Room Press' *Light Anthology,* where some of the poems in this book were first published.

Thanks to my beta readers, Lisette Auton and Alice Frecknall, who supplied me with the encouragement and intelligent questions I needed. I owe a huge debt to my superb editor Amy Acre, who is an exceptionally gifted reader of others' work and is in fact co-creator of this book.

CPSIA information can be obtained
at www.ICGtesting.com
Printed in the USA
BVHW082006071221
623424BV00007B/657